IN THE LONELY HOURS

Paul K Dolman

**A collection of poetry
and song lyrics**

ISBN:
978-1-7392664-0-0

Dedicated to

My sons: Joshua and Jacob Dolman,
Each aside of me.
With love and affection

And beautiful friends

Geoff French
&
Frederick Smithers

Both, too soon gone, but always
remembered.

Foreword

Some of the poems and songs in this collection appeared in my first attempt at publishing my own poetry in book form. It was called 'Under Spanish Skies'. If you bought it, you were one of fifty or so people to do so and for that I thank you. Actually, they say if you sell more than 50 copies of a poetry book, you're a runaway success!

But joking apart, I enjoyed the process of writing the poems and the fairly complex process of self-publishing. And because it was my first attempt and I lacked some of the necessary skills to do it well, it contained its share of errors. Thankfully errors that, in the end, did not seem to distract too much from the intended purpose of the poems themselves: to connect with the reader, to observe and bring alive life experiences, to explore and share facets of my own life and, finally, to move the reader to further explore the amazing and transforming world of poetry. A world where more established poets have proven that magical words laid out in a certain order, rhyming or not, short or long, can capture the ephemeral nature and fragility of life itself.

With all this in mind, I wanted to build upon and expand on my previous attempt. In this new book there are 15 new additional poems and six new songs lyrics.

This book is also being published in tandem with a music album, both being called 'In the Lonely Hours'. The idea was to also do an album and set some of the poems to music. As a result, five of the poems from the book are on the album, four of which have original music and arrangements by a good friend, Jason Newton. The fifth poem has original music by me and arranged by Jason. The album is also to showpiece the songs I have written. I don't profess to be great musician or singer but I believe the songs have some merit and in some way are an extension of my poetic ambitions.

As for the title I wanted to pinpoint the moment when my creativity takes places. In the main, the thoughts and ideas that are delivered to me are done so when I feel most alone. Sometimes, even when in the company of others, I have a feeling of solitude, of being on the outside. It is in these, usually quiet and contemplative times, that I am gripped by a desire to express myself.

But, even in these moments, I have to listen hard, open the gates to the mind and then exercise discipline to gather my thoughts and write down the words or chords that mysteriously enter.

But then this begs the question of why. Why poetry? Why any form of art? Do we need poetry? I think one of the best answers to this question was given by the acclaimed actor Ethan Hawke who said, and I paraphrase;

"Most people don't spend a lot of time thinking about poetry. Right? They have a life to lead... until their father dies, they go to a funeral, their child dies, somebody breaks your heart they don't love you anymore... and all of a sudden, you're desperate for making sense out of this life... and has anyone ever felt this bad before? How did they come out of this cloud?
Or the inverse.
You meet someone and your heart explodes. You love them so much you can't even see straight! You know, you're dizzy, did anyone feel like this before? What is happening to me....?
That's when art's not a luxury.
It's actually sustenance.
We need it."

So, on that note, if any of the words in this collection provides even a single morsel of sustenance, then my efforts will have been worth it.

- Paul K Dolman

The poems

Hijo Mio (Son of Mine)
(For my son Jacob)

In my self-enforced exile
one of my troops comes to give succour.
Cursed or blessed I have agonised on his behalf,
but the osmosis that takes place is undeniable.
Our animation and silences are in almost
synchronisitry,
while our hearts unfold
lIke un-crumpled red napkins.
This is not new, it has always been so,
for he is, a hijo mio.

Each, in our own way, suppresses
any ugliness in our lives,
with the beauty of the written word,
the inner scape of the moving image,
and the magic of notes on a page,
transformed into an auditory balm.

Now we walk the old streets of this Mallorca town,
in another mutual quest for beauty.
Our talk is quiet, sometimes desultory,
but always pointed.
We carry our hurts and wear our scars
ever so lightly,
never quite hardening into censure or reproach.

But what jaundiced cynicism I hold
are like bows and arrows to his
Gatling gun of youth and sense of fairness.
I salute him and surrender,
knowing that he is not only a hijo mio
but also, hijo de su madre.

Our love of the troubadour, the misfit and the
outsider ironically bring us together
and succour has been found.
The two of us are solitary by nature,
loving beauty when we find it,
a wound and its pain healed by the greyer life.
But when the wound opens,
we bleed together,
blood mingles
and we are renewed
and remade,
for he is,
a hijo mio.

Written in Mallorca 2018 after attending a Damian Rice concert.

Battle Fatigue

Once again, I am chastened by a memory of you,
re-filling my hollowed-out heart and bringing me to
my mental knees.
The gods ignore the pleas of the guilty,
intent on sending synaptic missiles.
And, for the moment, I surrender.

But this battle is worth losing
if I get to see your face one more time,
knowing eventually, time will win this war
and our love will be a mere corpse,
in our own poppy field.

Seeing us sharing the morning sun,
looking up at your undulating form, kaleidoscopic
light through your cascading hair, I feel an exquisite
pain, stabbing into me an erotic interlude, invading
and dissecting, my drab office day.

I am a lamb to the slaughter and should fight back,
with the tactic of a diversionary lack of grace.
But grace is all I have in this moment
and complete surrender is assured.
Forgive me for the coward I am.
I was neither the hero then,
or now.

From God's Own Garden
(Del Propio Jardín de Dios)

I sit and reap the reward,
relieved from nature's hoard.
My full and plundering hand,
picked from this bountiful land,
Del propio jardín de Dios.

Formed by elements and un-nurtured soil,
a masterpiece grown without man's toil
fruits hanging on trees bowed,
orphans, in meadows all bestowed,
from God's own garden.

Sun and light glistens on bleeding sap,
and, being a bee's favourite trap,
I carefully hide this golden treasure,
eating a few for immediate pleasure,
from God's own garden.

And in the taking there is a delight,
guiltless of creating a barren sight,
learning to consume only what I need,
in a world of voracious greed,
from God's own garden.

Spurning and in-different to earth's intrinsic gift,
avarice forever increasing man and nature's rift.
And never was it in dispute to take just our share,
but surely to co-exist in all life is but fair.
So, if the earth is at death's door,
Is it time to learn less is more?
From God's own garden.

Another Villanelle for Our Time
(A tribute to Leonard Cohen)

When the troubadours in our own times sing
And the poets' poems are recited,
To the feast of life, it's the wine they bring,
Changed from the water's well where words spring.
Then the fire in our hearts is reignited
When the troubadours in our times sing,
Ban the old prophets and hear new bells ring,
Let grace rise and polemics be benighted.
To the feast of life, it's the wine they bring.
Cadence diminishes all the fears that cling.
What passes for art, pricked and deflated
When the troubadours in our times sing.
The gift of poetics lifted by truths wing –
Even after the saviour is long departed,
To the feast of life, it's the wine *he* brings.
In the hearts of subjects, *he* remains king.
Offering no belief but only beauty intended
When the troubadour of our own time sings
To the feast of life, it's the wine *he* brings.

15

Entanglement

Entangle me into your life,
He once said
Let the frontiers be crossed
And oceans of discovery sailed.
Would they be savaged by the natives?
Or drowned by hurricanes?
He didn't care.
Entangle me into your life,
He once said
Let mountains be travailed
And jungles hacked through.
Would they be weary with the climb?
Or lose themselves in dense forests?
He didn't care.
Entangle me into your life,
He once said
For entanglement is the great adventure
Of advancing years
And loneliness is the dark expanse
Of the night sky
Offering remote possibilities
Of bumping into stars.
Knowing all this, he occasionally
Longed to be disentangled
For a gentle stroll
Of inward reflection
To have tea
On a sofa
For one.

16

Spanish Enclave

The tables have turned
And I've found my own enclave.
It is no accident I am here
But it feels unhurried and unforced.
Now, surrounded by Spanish campo,
I sit under a single almond tree
Where drupe and soul mature as one,
Fed by dappled and persistent sunlight.
An orchestra of cicadas
Play their opus of a single note.
Their maestro, the gentlest of breezes,
Lulls me into a rare unguarded reverie.
A sublime moment, captured
And surrounded by a hundred busy hours.

17

GoodSouls

(Inspired and dedicated to Fred & Denise Smithers)

Late in life I realise
I am on a constant search,
Crystallising from hope to belief.
It's always been just
Beneath the surface,
Of my ill-at-ease stance:
Behind the eyes of suspicion,
Seeking life's GoodSouls.

My religious experience?
My political nirvana?
My Atlantis and Eldorado?
My reddest red-letter day?
This is when I meet life's GoodSouls.

Move to the front of my stage,
It's not too crowded out there.
Many acts have come and gone,
But talent is remembered,
Take a bow and blow a kiss,
There will be many encores,
Long before my curtain falls,
For I have found more GoodSouls.

My religious experience?
My political nirvana?
My Atlantis and Eldorado?
My reddest red-letter day?
This is when I meet life's GoodSouls.

Haikus 1, 2 and 3

Haiku 1

For my dying friend,
Grant countless tomorrows' grace,
Or halt time's cruel race.

Haiku 2

Haunted dreams torment
Battled by black knights-errant,
Vanquished by sunrise.

Haiku 3

Beneath the tree's shade
Leaves sway 'gainst cobalt canvas,
Breeze kiss, yogic pose.

My Vista
(For Karen)

I stumble into each dawn,
eyelids unsticking, focusing
stretching out locked limbs.
When I look across to you,
your sleeping form and gentle presence,
in place and heart, raises not just
my head from my siren pillows,
but my dampened soul too.
Each morning I am reassured
to see your face and body again,
as I lose you to the night's darkness
but capture you again at morning light.

We are not everything we want of each other;
it's our private joke.
No eyes locked together across crowded rooms,
no chance encounter on a deserted shore,
no one-hundred impassioned letters
over the lifetime of a week.

No, not everything we want,
but everything we need.
Our joy of coming together is partly
borne out of our cancelled soap operas.

So, in our newly-found play
we are re-cast and re-scripted,
and we play for private laughs
knowing we will have the last ones.

Now, at the end of each of our discovered days,
my wounded heart beats a path to our door.
I'm sheltered by your smile
and warmed by the fire in your eyes.

In this house of love, we bid farewell to lives lost,
letting history's storms pass over.
We will climb our new mountain together
and in awe I will turn to you,
my new world view stretching out before me,
my landscape,
my vista,
my love.

Certainties

Truth is *your* truth
wherever you find it.
The only certainty is
That there is no certainty.
There is light in darkness
And darkness in light.
Fall to your knees and supplicate
To the God of ambiguity.
Seek your guidance here...
Or maybe there.
Wherever you find it,
Never believe your truth
Trumps others' truth.
As we get older, our certainties
Become ragged around the edges,
Eventually dissolving before our
Rheumy eyes.
I am certain of this,
Believe me,
It's true.

What We Think We Know

After all that I have learned, said and done
I believe I know less now than I did then.
All my thoughts and polemics that were hard-won
Are now the grave dust of dead men.

No matter, it's our right to be known and be heard
Given to us by a mysterious divine,
Yet wisdom attained will always be flawed
For true omniscience is an impossible line.

Baucis and Philemon
(Jenni and John Gregory)

In the forest of life, two young saplings
grew just inches apart.
Nourished by a goodness of soil,
they both took root,
determinedly taking hold.

In time, their young supple limbs reached
skyward, pushed upward by
warmth and light.

In proximity and a shared nature they grew
inexorably closer,
each compelled by love, desire and need,
until the saplings became entwined, a single entity,
becoming one in strength and surety.

In their inosculation, they shed seedlings
that, in turn, also grew toward the light.
Their now hardened limbs
giving protection to all below,
even seedlings blown in by an ill wind,
nurtured to grow tall and find a direction,
seeking their own horizon.

Now, in the blink of a cosmic eye,
one has withered, lost too soon.
But in the mirror of life, they reflect the myth of
Baucis and Philemon.

In their nature and fate
they will remain entwined in spirit,
that no death can put asunder.
For they, too, were favoured by the Gods,
for steadfastness, generosity,
hospitality to strangers
and for their recognition of divinity.

And so, their pitcher of love refills each day,
by courtesy of the Gods,
constantly watering those deep roots
that ensure they will, forever,
remain entwined.

*Philemon and Baucis, in Greek mythology, a pious Phrygian couple who
hospitably received Zeus and Hermes when their richer neighbours turned
away the two gods, who were disguised as wayfarers.*

This Spain!

This Spain!
Its margin beaches of pointed umbrellas
accuse the blatant sun.
And *alcazabas* pierce blue skies with
turrets stained by the black oil of death.

This Spain!
Once invaded by
Romans and
Goths
enslaving for land
and wealth,
now conquered
by modern
pleasure seekers
worshipping sun,
sea and sand.

This Spain!
Where Jew, Christian and Moslem
bartered in markets for cultural trinkets,
slaying and slaughtering on history's battlefields
for dogma and doctrine.

This Spain!
Cathedrals of gold are built on the bones
of conquered millions,
and the hubris of sailors willing
to sail past the world's edge.

This Spain!
That dances on the grave of flamenco
with gauche street moves
and sonorous arpeggios of nylon strings
engulfed by the strum of steel chords.

This Spain!
Captivating the literary hearts and minds
of Hemingway and Lee,
their zeitgeist passion made permanent
by blackened pages.

This Spain!
That birthed, celebrated and killed
their greatest presaging poet,
locking eyes with death
from the towers of Córdoba.

This Spain!
Where the ghost of Franco still silently haunts
the dreams and faces
of the ancient.
And mass graves
slowly reveal
the secret hatreds of *Familia* versus *Familia*.

This Spain!
At times too hasty to shrug off
its rich and colourful robes,
in its eagerness to dress in suits
of blandness and modernity.

This Spain!
Where Goya and Velazquez sublimely competes
with anonymous street graffiti,
and *La música de Rodriguez*
is drowned out by omnipresent euro pop.

This Spain!
That for centuries has lived
under the shadow of the seven hills,
slowly emerging into the sunlight
of emancipation and indifference.

This Spain!
Its land drenched in opulent light
and melancholic darkness,
cursed with abundance
and scarcity in equal measure.

This Spain!
Land of lush mediaeval forests, a vast desert
resembling the moon on earth,
flowing *rios de agua* and dusty riverbeds
snaking pointlessly to the sea.

This Spain!
Where the bull and the matador circle
warily into a forced uneasy truce,
but the spirit of Don Quixote still tilts
at imaginary and real enemies.

This Spain!
Of fiestas, in their exuberance posturing a
joyful presence and hopeful future,
persistently trying to
exorcise a sorrowful past.

This Spain!
The Iberian Peninsula of jagged mirrors
reflecting multitudes of traits and paradoxes;
where, in a millennia or two, millions lost
and found themselves:
this is SPAIN!

Esta España...
(Translated by Jesus Contreras)

Esta España...
Con sus playas que abundan en
puntiagudas sombrillas culpando a
un sol insolente;
con sus alcazabas, que penetran
en los cielos azules...
con sus torreones
manchados por el aceite
negro de la muerte.

Esta España...
Donde el espectro de
Franco aún persigue en
silencio
los sueños y los
semblantes de los más
ancianos;
donde los enterramientos
masivos aún desvelan el
odio intestino entre familias.

Esta España...
Donde la sublimidad de Goya y de Velázquez
compiten con grafitis callejeros anónimos;
donde la música del maestro Rodrigo se ahoga
bajo la omnipresencia del lamúsica pop.

31

Esta España...
Con sus doradas catedrales construidas sobre los
huesos de millares de sometidos;
y la soberbia de sus marinos ansiando navegar
más allá del borde del mundo.

Esta España...
La que ahora baila sobre la tumba del flamenco al
son de chabacanos bailes callejeros;
la que ahoga los sonoros arpegios de cuerdas de
nailon por el rasgueo de las de acero.

Esta España...
La que cautivó los corazones de Hemingway y de
Lee;
y su pasión por el espíritu del tiempo fue eternizada
en páginas ya hoy ennegrecidas.

Esta España..
Donde el toro y el matador giran con cautela
alrededor de una complicada tregua.
Pero el espíritu de Don Quijote todavía se inclina
a enemigos imaginarios y reales.

Esta España...
Que vio nacer, celebró e igualmente mató al más
grande y presagiador de sus poetas,
atissbando cómo la muerte le buscaba desde las
torres de Córdoba.

Esta España...
La invadida por romanos y godos que la
esclavizaron por sus riquezas; la que ahora ha sido
conquistada por los veneradores del sol y de la
playa.

Esta España...
Tan esmerada en otros tiempos en las chaquetillas
y en las batas de colores;
y tan tan perdida hoy en sus nuevas vestimentas de
blanda modernidad.

Esta España...
La que durante siglos ha vivido bajo la sombra de
las siete colinas;
la que ha emergido lentamente hacia la luz de su
emancipación y de la indeferencia.

Esta España...
Empapada de opulenta luminosidad y de
melancólica oscuridad;
maldecida por igual con la abundancia como con la
escasez.

Esta España...
Donde judíos, cristianos y musulmanes hacían
trueques de baratijas en los mercados e
intercambio de culturas. Matando y asesinando en
históricos campos de batalla en nombre de sus
dogmas y doctrinas.

Esta España...
Tierra de exhuberantes bosques medievales, un
vasto desierto que recuerda a la luna, arroyos y
polvorientas ramblas que serpentean incansables
hacia el mar.

Esta España...
La de las Fiestas, en su exhuberancia creativa de
un gozoso presente y esperanzador futuro,
persistentemente intentando olvidar y exorcizar un
apesadumbrado pasado,

Esta España...
La península ibérica de espejos escarpados que
reflejan un millar más de atributos y paradojas.
Donde en un milenio o dos, millones
se han perdido y se han encontrado
Esta es ESPAÑA.

Today We Pushed the Limits of Our Hearts

....and each time we do it takes longer
to snap back into that ideogram of our
collective psyche.

It's a rigid organ at best, calcifying,
over a lifetime of beating slower
to love's rhythm.

Again, your perfectionism shines a light
into the deep recesses of my imperfections.
I am like a rabbit, wide-eyed and found wanting,
caught in the glare, of your expectation.

But then I react with a wearisome fury,
a lifetime of seemingly disappointing those who
say they care for me.
In that very same fury, I hear myself crash onto
the jagged rocks of self-pity.

Self-harm to the soul is less visible
and harder to heal,
unlike the scabs of inadequacies picked,
knowingly or otherwise,
by that special other.

I Hold You Dearest of all my Friends

You have comforted me in my darkest hours
and waited in the shadows of lighter ones.
You never allowed me to sink
into self-pity or despair.

A constant from my earliest days, growing in loyalty
and subtlety as I grew in age and acceptance.
I never had to summon you: you always found me,
my sanities' safety net.
And so, I hold you dearest of all my friends
............I hold you dearest of all my friends.

Of course, you lost me other friends
and even lovers of mine grew tired of you,
enamour eventually soured to disenchantment.
You have been misunderstood all your life,
chastised and denied affirmation
and slandered with different names.
Slowly, you taught me to understand who you really
are.
And so, I hold you dearest of all my friends
............I hold you dearest of all my friends.

Who can boast of a friend that guided them
through savage experience into
learned empathy and compassion?
Who taught me to see beauty in the mundane?
You did all that for me.

Educating and counselling me,
elevating soul and consciousness,
simply by being just you.
And so, I hold you dearest of all my friends.
… .... I hold you dearest of all my friends.

At times, in my immaturity,
I tried to disown you and push you away,
embarrassed by your presence.
We all try, at times, to be something we are not;
I know you have forgiven me for those lapses
because you are still by my side, certain you will be
with me when I take my final breath.
And so, I hold you dearest of all my friends
… .... I hold you dearest of all my friends.

But forgive me for my rudeness,
I have not formally introduced you,
but should say you have met many times before.
Meet my good friend melancholia…
the one I hold dearest of all my friends.

The one I hold dearest of all my friends.

Dance With Me

Let me take your hand,
leading you to the water's edge.
I'll dance with you
under the moonlit sky,
a private and joyful silhouette
against a dark and painful backdrop
Let us throw our heads back
and abandon the world,
You and I linked at the hips,
will thresh our own circle in the sand.
Grace closes the space that has kept us apart
and in the heat of the dance
we will melt into each other's arms.
And lying together where the sea and sand meet,
asking no questions and answering with no lies,
exhausted and spent, we will be cooled and
anointed by each breaking wave.
For us only, the moon will dissolve
into falling confetti of pure light,
celebrating this wondrous,
but temporary, union of body and soul.
And tomorrow we can say our goodbyes.

The Death of Fear

Do you ever contemplate and fear
your final day?
How, and where, it will be?
The date, the hour, the minute and the second?
Perhaps now is the time?

Morbid, some would say.
But death is the black shadow, lengthening
as the sun sinks lower.
The same shadow that whispers
and haunts the corners of the mind,
louder and more visible each passing year.

Morbid, some would say.
But as it has been said before,
it is as sure as the payment of taxes,
and 'choice' is not a word in Death's vocabulary.

So perhaps, now is the time?
To meditate on it, think on it,
accept its inevitability and fear it no more.
Then this rough gem of a life can be polished
into a diamond that is
smooth to the heart,
hardens the mind,
dazzles and blinds the soul,
to the fleeting nature of who we are.

Do you ever contemplate and fear
your final day?
How, and where, it will be?
The date, the hour, the minute and the second?
Now is the time.

Desertion

You, always one for sitting at the captain's table,
while all at sea, I was plainly the mate less able.
Where were you when storms hit and the boat went
down?
While I, out there in cold waters, left to drown,
You, striking for the land with a compass, on life's-
boat,
Me grasping for air and the wreckage to stay afloat.

You were one of my troops standing close to my side;
when the enemy came, there was nowhere to hide.
Over the top we went at the officer's command,
but too soon we were separated in no man's land.
And where were you when the enemy started to fire?
Safe in a foxhole while I hung from the barbed wire.

But these are the grand stories, I hear you say,
asking, *when were you deserted and in what way?* Is
pain and emptiness less if the story is small? Lovers
who leave, walking, never returning your call.
Or powerless playground children snubbed by so-
called friends,
spending a lifetime trying to please and make amends

Of wives and husbands who leave
a stale marriage bed,
tired of lives they lead,
preferring others instead.

But whether the loss is big or small,
or we stand straight or on bellies crawl.
Desertion is not something we can avoid
unless you're willing to live in the void

So don't fear what may be or even try to keep a
score,
it's preparing you for the biggest betrayal of all.
As we all stumble blindly down life's corridor,
passing scarred, but elegiacally through that final
door.

Athina

A city it would seem where all wear black
Each tainted by their own Greek tragedy.
Graffitied buildings now symbols of despair
People's toothless political remedy

Denizens too restless to sleep,
Side by side in soulful moods of long decay
Buffeted and bowed by fresh new winds,
Hoping to blow in just one untainted day.

With empty eyes, police stand bored and smoke
Dutifully defending corner streets
Their shields, gas masks and batons at the ready
We to cool and bourgeois to leave our seats.

We witness tear gases for the masses
Foretold by that now unloved poet, once read
Yet the diners nervously stay, laugh and eat
Unsure if any of the hungry have yet fled

But then when the bangs and screams begin
We're encouraged to move inside
When we leave, eyes smart, throats faintly burn,
Searching the ground; under police eyes

City of joy and pain, all on display
Will you slow the tempo of this decline?
Remembering your once glorious past
Tasting again like the finest Greek wine.

43

Ta Léme our Athina, your once famed beauty
Has surely dimmed and faded over time,
But to survey your worldly influence
From the Acropolis is worth the climb.

Perhaps the Gods will return one bright day
And fierce Zeus will again sit on his throne,
Changing Athena's fate, to be no longer
The prose shadow to the poem that is Rome.

The Journey In-Between

This was when maxis and minis were skirts and cars,
Before Zimmerman sold his soul for an electric guitar.

Born nineteen years after the Second World War,
A baby boomer mistake of nineteen sixty-four.

Though the bond between mother and child was torn
It was never something I would really mourn.

Ringo and George were not the names to call,
Your children would be either John or Paul.

So, the latter forever became my moniker,
For this less than famous autobiographer.

Saved from foster homes and
possible evil within,
I was luckier than many with my
newly-found kin.

Earnest and Katherine opened
their home and hearts –
For this rejected child no more
stop and starts.

I kept my smile and dimples
and a heart without much fear
Only occasionally shedding a
pitiful tear

Walsall was my home, Bloxwich the town to be precise
A Black Country estate not known for its culture and sights

The roots from which a boy could be loved into a man,
Where respect and values born out of sacrifice began.

I joined public libraries getting my books for free,
happy in my bedroom with Hobnobs and tea.

I dreamed of far exotic places and romantic travel
Waiting for puberty and childhood to slowly unravel

On street corners I would hang with Pezza and Baker,
Sometimes by the off-licence and perhaps the chip shop
later.

Football, music and girls our topics of conversation;
No understanding of what went on in the nation.

And weekends with Mozza learning to play guitar,
Watching Top of the Pops, hoping to be a star.

But mainly times alone, playing music and reading books,
Checking spots in mirrors and wishing for better looks.

My parents were children of that Victorian age:
At odd times we read from a different page.

In my twenties, I watched them go grey and die
For all they did, deep within my heart, they will lie.

Now I've fed my desire and
travelled far and wide,
But remember Walsall and my
beginnings with pride.

For wherever you begin your life
and what it might mean,
May well determine your end
and the journey in- between.

The Battlefield That is Love

We marched almost a lifetime,
until we finally met on the battlefield.
Terms were offered and declined.
So, we warred and battled,
and then sued for peace.
When the truce broke we warred and battled again.
And, in the heat of combat,
when my head was turned away from you,
you plunged your soul into mine.

Deeply wounded,
I surrendered, and with no fight left in me,
you captured my heart
taking it as your own.
Now I am yours, with no desire
to escape or do battle again.
Content to be your prisoner
for the lifetime we have left.

Forgiving Knowledge

To my heart:
Forgive me for when I've failed,
Forgive me for when I withdrew,
And for not keeping you nourished
With ones that were honest and true.

To my soul:
Forgive me for being human,
Forgive me for just being you...
I started with the best intentions
but my virtues were all too few.

To my mind:
Forgive me for not finding my purpose quicker,
Forgive me for insight that only slowly grew
For lacking the instinct and empathy
That may well have grown the heart and soul too

Forgive me for not finding my purpose quicker
Forgive me for insight that only slowly grew
But finally finding this self-knowledge in me
Has made me a better man than one or two

Homeless

Do I doubt this was once a kingly man
who now sits on a cardboard throne?
Do I wonder how this once portentous child lost his
innocent smile?
If the breath he inhales is oxygen of hope,
his exhale is carbon dioxide of despair?
Do I consider the journey he has made?
Understanding only that he is lost and unfound
in the present wastelands of his life
Can I bear to hear his coughs and splutters, as if
choking on his own troubles?

Do I feel the weight of his head hung low,
pulled down by human indifference?
And when he lifts lids as heavy as dead-weights,
do I quickly glimpse eyes as empty as when the
soul has fled a lifeless body?
All this comes crashing into my mind
in that split second that I walk on by,
averting my eyes, before it could possibly
make any difference
to either him
or I.

Reflections in Our Children's Eyes

Well, I followed all the rules
Sharing a piece of my life
With a surprising young girl
Who agreed to be my wife.

I clocked in at nine
And finished at five,
We talked about our day
Thinking we were alive.

We built a home on rock
That quickly changed to sand
Losing all that we had
To fate's sleight of hand.

I smiled whenever she frowned;
She frowned whenever I smiled.
The emotions in-between
Never being reconciled.

Soon these lovers turn to enemies
Killing the love, like many before,
But these stories rarely just stop there
As creating life means you give more

Now the seasons have all quickly passed
And the seeds sown are mature and grown
Sons, wearing the fragile mantle of adults,
Finding their way, making mistakes of their own.

I have no regrets of lives led before
And so, racing down these last few years
I have learned that the chemistry of love
Is formed through pain, joy, laughter and tears.

And despite all the pledges, failings and lies,
We stay as reflections in our children's eyes.

Hometown

Bloxwich, it's not a name that rolls off the tongue.
Syllables giving a perception that's wrong

A place that's not loved like a treasured locket
More like loose change rattling in God's own pocket

But housing estates full of salt of the earth,
Where people mine deep to find their self-worth

Homes built just after the war, some grey and stark
With oasis's of greens to play and king George's park

Thatched Cottage, Sir Robert Peel and other pubs
Easing life's fears with chat, beer and Sunday grub

It's where family comes first for the vast majority
With no side we talk with sometime brutal sincerity

But it's community is what keeps us together,
Any ignorance swapped by our own type of 'clever'

You may think that it's a place time has forgotten
Perhaps by those that left? Then you'd be forgiven!

For if you were born and lived as a Bloxwegian,
You're shaped by the very best of this region

And there is a pride that requires no need to brag:
We just quietly let Bloxwich fly its own flag

Hunter of the Interior Heart

I am a hunter of the interior heart,
stalking and foraging in famine,
setting traps by night and day,
sometimes marching, other times crawling
on my empty belly, into unknown territories.
Forays that occasionally result in sustenance
and, though fleeting, stave off long days
of thirst and hunger.

Not content with the ordinary spoils
of this war against life,
I have wanted to crack shells,
peel skins,
and hunt prey.
But victories are few and rare
and mostly I am the victim of constant counterattack
of those camouflaged mercenaries of cliche, vacuity
and conformity.

Hunt with me, it's never too late,
our diminishing callowness is our greatest weapon.
And perhaps the greatest pleasure lies
in the hunting itself: experience has taught me,
even the thought of the prey is worth the wait.

As for danger, that only lies in never hunting at all.
For when we capture those moments,
making our kill, we will learn to chew more slowly
and savour every flavour of these rare banquets.

And though only satiated for a while,
we will continue and be content to know we are,
hunters of the interior heart.

Humanity

The Little Owl died in your hands tonight.
A mini tragedy that unveiled the fragility of nature
and our undeniable connection with it.

When the soul fled from its trembling body, it took a
part of us with it. Your compassion, embracing its
last heart beats, seemed to envelope us all, lifting
us out of our selfish selves.

Luck was not on its side, as it leapt from the
roadside into the side of our car on that moonlit and
lonely Spanish back road. Stunned on impact, you
compelled us to turn back. Defying our feeble
justifications to press on. Determined to help, you
sought it out: prone and helpless, susceptible to the
savagery of car wheels.

As we drove through the night, I sensed your silent
prayers as you nursed it in your healing hands.
If only you could have shared your life force.

But as you examined it under the harsh light of home,
searching for broken wings and a possible Lazarus
within, it convulsed one last time, its little head lolling
in defeat.

As its heart stopped, all our pulses slowed in a
collective salute, our only comfort this:
it didn't perish alone by the roadside,
but in your warm, considerate, comforting hands and
witnessed by that increasingly rarest of all loves,
Humanity.

Let Me Tell You the Truth About Love

Let me tell you the truth about love:
It's '*all around*', '*here, there or everywhere*'.
There's a '*story*' and its '*endless*'.
Though '*hard to find*', '*it's in the air…*'

We're always chasing and hounding it,
Perhaps out of a dark and hidden despair?
Jealous of the lucky who have found it
As it is a lie, that love, like war is fair.

Now it seems love is about what you say,
Never the things that you *ought* to do.
Confusing some of a certain gender,
Making the mistake they thought they knew.

Is love a catchphrase for all that we like?
Or only the reserve of God above?
Perhaps, but if you keep an open mind,
I'll tell you the truth about love.

Okay, let me tell you the truth about love:
It's giving and not quite getting back.
Of being surrounded by darkness
But seeing light through the crack.

Allowing yourself time to be alone,
Never giving into your despair.
Searching to find it deep within,
Before you even begin to share

You cannot force, hold it or make it stay,
Though you think it fits just like a glove.
You cannot prove it by giving a ring
Or through the act of setting free a dove.

But don't listen to what I say or espouse
Perhaps it is none of the above
As more experienced 'prophets' will proclaim:
"We can tell you the truth about love."

I'm Dying up Here

I'm driven by insane fear of remaining unknown.
But it's all of my own making, let it be made clear,
Making myself vulnerable for the world to see
But the big question is, will I be dying up here?

Facebook or Instagram or any virtual stage
And with no eyes to witness, there is still no less fear:
I'll still be sweating, my stomach in creative knots
'cause let's face it I could still end up dying up here!

Have I got something new to say, I'm never too sure
Will the crowd clap loudly, boo or jeer? (not that I'll
hear)
Am I the born storyteller I believe I am?
With no real feedback, I'm think I'm dying up here.

Of course, I'm honing my craft, improving every day
Yearning for more than a 'like' from a poetic peer
Sure I'm wasting my time, even deluding myself:
Everyone's signed off and I'm already dead up here!

The Actors

To many plot twists
brings confusion to any tale.
Fluffed lines and missed cues
making each leading actor fail

Both now playing for different
applause from the crowd
Surprised hy jeers and bous
turning from whispers to loud

The lonely stage brings new
understudies to the fore
The main attractions leave
quietly by the stage door.

With no chance to rehearse
but still passion to perform
Ending badly when the critics
reviews were lukewarm

"They lacked chemistry….."
"Acting   and   story   not   top   drawer
…despite the weight of literature that's gone
before"

Early ending of another play is of no surprise.
As the actors start one wo/man shows with this
play's demise.

The Bookends of Our Days

Know that these are the bookends of our days
Holding the stories of billions of lives
No one knows how many chapters we have
Only the knowledge no one survives.

Do we get a choice of our own genre?
Streams of consciousness or precise prose?
Are we characters living out contrived plots,
In the image of an author no one knows?

Are you one of the rich few or among the many poor,
Under the impressionistic cover of being free?
And though our plots may flow, are our stories just
cliché,
Unfolding due to the accident of geography?

Mystery, comedy or tragedy, we'll not know –
Just like novels, events can turn on a single phrase
It's the Start and the End we can be most certain of
For Birth and Death will be the bookends of all our
days.

Foster Mother: That's How I Remember it Anyway

When I ran my hand through my thin hair and said,
"I'm going to go bald,"
you simply replied,
"Yes, probably."
We were emphatic in our agreement, though you
never saw my prophesy come true.
That's how I remember it anyway.

In a rare moment
of tenderness and pride, you said,
"You have come-to-bed eyes,"
a quality,through my life I never fully exploited,
nor one I found reflected back to me in the mirror.
That's how I remember it anyway.

On your birthday, I cycled my chopper bike in my
favourite woollen tank top
and bought you a single bone China teacup.
You hugged me and said into my ear,
"That's lovely. Thank you."
One of the few but treasured hugs you gave me.
That's how I remember it anyway.

In my teens, sitting by the fire with a towel
half-around me, you said,
"You'll make a girl happy one day."
In my innocence I only understood years later.
That's how I remember it anyway.

When we battled, I had to have the final word. You
would say,
"You have an answer for everything!"
But I just thought I did and life showed me otherwise.
That's how I remember it anyway.

Helping you to sit up with cushions behind your back,
you would whisper, stoically, with empty eyes and
shortness of breath,
"Thank you."
I would turn away as tears would slip from my eyes
That's how I remember it anyway.

And when on the phone to a friend,
I heard the words shouted by my father,
"She's gone."
I ran into the sitting room, throat constricted; through
blurry eyes saw you had slipped away.
That's how I remember it anyway.

This was thirty five or more years ago.
Your name was Katherine;
you took me in, cared and loved me,
That's how I remember it anyway.

Parting

'Till death us do part':
So states one manifest for union,
But parting can happen before many a death
No 'raging against the dying of the light' here –
Only, for some, where once was love,
A slow unchecked extinguishing
Now, but more then, spontaneous shafts of light
Pierce the dark recesses of the heart:
Illuminating, but no longer meaningful.
The fabric of their lives gossamer thin,
Stretched tightly, ready to snap.
In public and private places, they have finally
Run out of things to say.
Grunts and nods
Now pass for the language of love

Parents of the Lost

When war comes,
at what age do we stop fearing for ourselves,
but instead for our sons and daughters?
The loss of their futures mourned
well before they have fallen,
willing to forfeit whatever time we have left
for what they could have.

I have no answer.
Only to scream out
in my living nightmare
to history's parents,
just to see responses
on their grave and gaunt faces
in sepia films and in faded print.

And of course, if it even mattered,
only hindsight informs,
with the musings of the victors,
as to whether it was 'justified'.
And that sacrifices made meant
they died as either heroes of purpose
or victims in vain?

We can try to protect them all their lives,
guardians of their hopes and dreams.
Only to lose them to machinations of power
beyond our control, or simply at the behest or
whim of a madman.

In our grief and self-pity, we plead out loud
to a history that only echoes back
with the silence of nothing learned.
Or we fall to our knees, imploring the empty skies,
But our only communion will always
and will only ever be
with the parents of the lost.

On Life's Outer Edges

Catch me on life's outer edges...
You'll find me now and then looking in.
but now, no longer enviously.
I am a sometimes-bemused bystander,
content to forge my own path,
having so often stumbled,
over stones of un-acceptance,
cleared weeds of discontent
and finding myself lost in darkness.
But now, rounding the corner,
I meet blindingly beautiful vistas
of self-fulfilment.
Warmed by a sun of a pure self-love,
and cooled by a breeze of thankfulness.
My soul restored,
I continue my journey,
on life's outer edges.
That's where you'll find me.
and, if you have a mind to,
come, join me.

September Spain

For eleven months nature's elements feed,
and nurture this pregnant and replete land.
In those early months, landscapes are slowly
painted with a lush verdant; trees burst into blossom,
feeding spring fruits, erupting and hanging
heavy on branches pulled closer to earth.

As time passes, a fierce sun emerges;
blistering, baking the earth's crust;
rays scorching all in its path.
The heat sends geckos scurrying, searching for the
darkness of holes and coolness of cracks.

On rare occasions, rain falls like a gentle tap dance,
dampening the ever-present dust.
At other times, returning, battering
with a tropical vengeance , a deluge of torrents,
gushing down mountainsides and cascading through
pueblos, cooling and cleansing in its wake, satiating
the throat of this now dry and thirsty land.

Unexpected breezes dance, brushing
and caressing sun-kissed skin.
Now and then loud and raucous winds
holler through the night,
rattling shutters and doors,
leaving its calling card of African dust,
blanketing the firmament.

Finally, full and rounded, Mother Earth
gives birth to its twelfth month; a ripened,
iridescent new-born of perfection;
beautifully formed and named,
September Spain.

In the Lonely Hours

I lie here, caught between the dying embers
of the night and the sparks of a new day.
The faces of lovers dance before my eyes,
And as many parallel, stunted and incomplete
dreams slowly diffuse they slowly settle like dust,
caught in shafts of the morning sun light, passing
through the bedroom window.

I stare through this glass of velvet wine it reflects
like a fractured mirror the hearth and fire that repels
my Autumn coldness.
For a while, I hold the fearless gaze of my
bedridden and dying mother and sense
the diminished heart of a defeated Father
staring into his own winter fire.

But the warmth of the life they lived courses through
my blood, like every sip I take of this full-bodied
Rioja that warms and engorges
my cooling heart.

In past times, on winter days I have walked
deserted shores barely able to discern where the
sea and sky meet on a horizon blurred by grey.

I have seen the tender
faces of my children appear
and fade with each
incoming and receding
wave. Now our lives
together are in the ebb
before low tide settles,
knowing one day there will
be one last high tide on this
particular but spectacular
beach.

In earlier days I have sat in the gloom of my dimly lit
bedroom, in the midnight hours, through what
seems like an endless childhood.

I am reading voraciously, itching to live out the
words that swim before my eyes. And as quickly as
one is finished, like the dying take a kiss, I reach
down from the shelf for another offering of love.

Now in these times, for many, past and future
collide, each competing for our mind space.
As time gathers pace future surrenders, little by
little, retreating into the past.

The known is preferred to the unknown, uncertainty
replaced by the safety of certainty. Future dreams
are traded for nostalgia and those *'better times'*.

But these are when the battles that take place and
are valiantly fought,
In the Lonely Hours,

when magic weaves its spell and art is born,
making permanent, in whatevor form or passion
captures our souls,
In the Lonely Hours,

when our hearts and minds stops, just for a
moment, to explore all that we have lost
or might gain,
In the Lonely Hours,

In the Lonely Hours.

Earlier poems

Hospital Bed
(A Sonnet

Here she sits with me in these times alone;
We speak of all that's said and left unsaid.
Cares and problems for years I would bemoan
are, with tender love and care, put to bed.

Now, medicated and waited upon,
with brittle bones and lined flesh that decays,
a once, bright active mind is all but gone,
looking out on a picture world of greys.

This instance I see her radiance too.
Reaching, she clasps my hand and holds it tight,
but my hand to touch her cheek passes through
and this old man weeps and gives up the fight.

My love, now gone, a spirit that has fled,
Or just a memory, inside my head?

My Children

Life sprang from me
Taking me by surprise.
Bestowing a burden of love,
Lighter each passing day.

But how can I ever hope
To meet the full measure of your expectations,
When I stumble to meet my own?

Answers lie in youth's elixir.
Your miracles of pain and hope
strip me bare of all pretensions and ego,
until I am a child again.
And then we are one,
My children and I.

The Unknown

I or you have a need inside
that goes well beyond any fear.
It reaches out, only to slip,
defeated, by futures unclear.

Where is the purpose
stretching beyond our self?
Though we may live longer
Our histories have less to tell

So back to the world we go,
its plainness we abhor.
Existence begs not the question
why? But *what* is it all for?

To eat and sleep
to work and play
to love and lose and
die little each day?

For gone are the big men,
and deeds of yesteryear,
and romantic worlds only exist
in an unknowns' fallen tear.

Adultery: Three Sides to Every Story

To one, the word is distant and unclear
Or constantly appealing.
To the other, the word never comes at all.

To one, the idea is laughable and inconceivable
Or brazenly enticing.
To the other, the idea never comes at all.

To one, the thought is insidious, corrupting,
Or guilefully attractive.
To the other, the thought never comes at all,

To one, the situation is coincidental and chance
Or planned rendezvous.
To the other, the situation never comes at all.

To one, the act is coy and flattering
Or gratuitously erotic.
To the other, the act never comes at all.

To one, the aftermath is guilt and remorse
Or shamelessly exhilarating.
To the other the aftermath is
All
    of
      the
          above.

I Am a Toaster

The toaster is faulty, it no longer functions.
To repair it would be a waste of time.
Throw it out.
Why waste time and effort repairing it
When it is easier to get a new one?
They are much cheaper now and nicely packaged.
They don't make them as well as they used to
And not as good value.
But this one, it looks old and battered, worn out.
It has lost its shine and now it's tarnished.
The new one will look and function better.
And people will admire it.
For a while.

Twelve songs

Restless In the Dawn

(A song inspired by the travel writer
Patrick Leigh Fermor)

You took me on a journey
Where the sun never sets.
You told me all your stories
Of places seen and people met.

I walked a thousand miles
Right there by your side,
And though I never knew you
Your words touched my mind.

*I will always be the man
Who's restless in the dawn
And wonders what wonders
Each day are born.*

*One of life's doors
That your soul
Gave the key...*

I'll climb those lonely mountains
And cross those stormy seas,
Gazing from castle turrets;
Sleeping under forest trees.

Learning from the great and small
Until I find my own way,
Reaching out for stranger's love –
In this battered heart, they'll stay.

I will always be the man
Who's restless in the dawn
And wonders what wonders
Each day are born.

One of life's doors
That your soul
Gave the key...

You haunt my dreams at night
And crowd my empty days,
Changing all the landscapes
In a hundred different ways.

And many years from now,
Taking you down from my shelf,
I'll read through misty eyes:
You've become part of myself.

I Will Always Feel This Way

(Written after the passing of my sister Angela and brother
Michael)

And the day is so short,
And day is so cold,
And I'm feeling my age,
And I am feeling so old.

But no one will know
How I really feel:
Though many have tried
No one has yet broken the seal.

And I guess it will always be this way,
And I will always feel this way.

But deep in my heart
There's a peace inside,
And when worlds caves in
It's where the soul hides.

No one can break
Either friend or foe
This heart of mine
The safest place I can go.

And I guess it will always be this way,
And I will always feel this way.

And it's the heart
That holds the grace,
So always keep a space
For those days when the world turns grey.

And it's the heart
That holds grace,
So always keep a space
For those days when the world turns grey.

Though the day is so short,
Though the day is so cold,
Though I'm feeling my age,
After all that is told…

I am at peace: it will always be this way,
And I'm at peace, I will always feel this way.

Where Broken Dreams go to Die

Is there a place
Where the sun never shines?
Where some of me
Is no longer mine?
Is it where broken dreams
Go to die?

They say that *the winner takes it all*
But pride comes before a fall
And I wanted it all for free
Without paying life's fee.

Perhaps, like the Phoenix, they'll rise
And take our enemies by surprise,
And so let the battles begin
It's just another war we need to win.

Take up your arms
And let's march awhile:
We'll win our future
Or lose with style.
Hold your nerve,
No more single file.

It's never too late
For us to learn to see
Thumb your nose at fate
And write your own destiny.
You just have to believe
One more time

Is there a place
Where the sun never shines?
Where some of me
Is no longer mine?
Is it where broken dreams
Fly again?
Is it where dreams can
Live again?

Reconciliation

Do you see
What I am seeing?
Do you believe
What I am believing?
And do you feel
What I am feeling?

Now I'm gone –
Are you sitting all alone,
Waiting for the phone
To ring?
Well, I'm lying in my bed
With an aching head
And no heart left to sing
And if the writing's on the wall
Then close up the door
Shut down the future
And hear no more.

Can I find
What is missing?
Can I mend
What is broken?
Can I heal
What is scarred?
Now you're gone.

Are you hiding from the sun
Now freedom has won the war?
Is it sorrow we gain
Or love's refrain
We want more?
And if the writing's on the wall
Then open up the door
Listen to the future
And hear love's call.

Do you know
What I'm knowing?
Can you tell
What I'm telling?
Can you sense
What I'm sensing
now it's gone?

Will the light shine
In the darkness?
Will the veil fall
From our eyes?
Will the head lose
And our hearts confess
One last time?
Can we believe,
One...
Last...
Time?

There For You
(For my son Joshua)

You can wrestle with the wind,
And make despair your friend.
You can sail against the tide
Asking yourself why happiness lied.

But remember
I'll always be there for you.

Seeing the frame, but never the picture.
Ever the watcher, but never the painter.
Expecting those around to disappoint,
Never quite seeing life's point.

But remember
I'll always be there for you,
I'll always be there for you.

And if the winter starts to descend
And your heart and mind are struggling to mend
Then put aside all your
Where's and your why's

For remember, you are the son that
Brightens up both our lives.

You are the son that brightens up both our lives

So, find the joy in every day
And believe me when I say:

I will always be there for you,
I will always be there for you,
Always for you.

If We Walk On by

Some of us living
But there's plenty more dying,
And for everyone whose smiling
There are too many crying.

But it's never gonna change,
And we'll always feel their pain
If we walk on by,
If we walk on by,
If we walk on by.

And some of us are healing
But there's countless others bleeding
And for everyone remembered
There are too many forgotten.

And if we never even try
Then we'll always hear their cry
If we walk on by,
If we walk on by,
If we walk on by.

And there's no guarantee
Of a problem-free sheet
And we could find ourselves
On the very same street.

Like a bitter pill
We may swallow our pride
'Cause behind the façade
There is nowhere to hide.

And with heads that are bowed
And a voice not too proud we
will whisper out loud...please,

Don't walk on by,
Please don't walk on by,
Please don't walk on by,
Please don't walk on by.

It's a Crazy World

Wake up now: don't sleep-walk.
It's time for action and no more talk
Coz when the sh… hits the fan
Time waits for no man.
Coz it's a crazy world
We all live in now
Don't know who and I don't know how,
Who's gonna take our hand
And lead us to the promised land?

Coz it's the crack and the drugs
And the crazy thugs,
It's the bombs and the wars
And millennial bugs.
It ought to be a dream
But all I wanna do is scream –
Yeah scream
And scream!

You gotta ask the questions
And determine the lies,
Listen to the people and hear their cries,
For when it all goes down
We need a leader not a clown.

Coz it's a crazy world that has lost its way
And we all seem to have a lot to say,
The tables are full at every venue
but truth's not on the menu.

Coz it's the crack and the drugs
And the crazy thugs,
It's the bombs and the wars
And millennial bugs.
It ought to be a dream
But all I wanna do is scream –
Yeah scream
And scream!

So, take my hand
And let's fly away
To another place
Where there's no...

Crack and drugs and crazy thugs
Bombs and wars
And millennial bugs.
It ought to be a dream
But all I wanna do is scream –
Yeah scream
And scream!

As Beautiful to Me

Guess I was a dreamer before
You passed before my eyes.
Guess I was a dreamer
Before you made me realise
Life is for the living
Not for dreaming away;
Life is for the taking,
Not for giving away.

Guess it's never gonna change
And I'll never ever see
Anyone as beautiful
As you were to me.

Anyone as beautiful to me
Anyone as beautiful to me
Anyone as beautiful to me

I guess I was a loser
Before you taught me how to find,
Guess I was a loser
Before you opened up my mind

To all the things that I should see
And to all the things I *could* be
For giving me the rest of my life,
But without you next to me.

Guess it's never gonna change
And I'll never ever see
Anyone as beautiful
As you were to me.

Don't Break This Spell

When you came into my life,
You shared all your grace,
You stopped me in my tracks
And gave me a sense of place.
Now I track the contours of your smile,
Seeing new horizons through your eyes.

Though I searched the world for beauty
And wide-open space,
I can now write a hundred poems
Simply about your face.

So, I ask the gods above: don't break this spell
'Cause when you're not here, heaven turns to hell.
You don't know where I've come from
And you don't know what I've been through,
But if I need to pass the test
Theb the answers
Lie with you.

And through a hundred lies
You gave me a choice.
I heard the single truth
Within in your voice:
I'd never realised
Perfection could be this real
Because what I cannot see
Is not what I feel.

And reality is not all that it seems,
When your love is a ghost of future dreams.

Of future dreams,
A ghost of future dreams.

So, I ask the gods above: don't break this spell
'Cause without my dreams
Heaven would be hell.
I won't know where you've come from
And I won't know what you've been through,
But if you need to pass the test
Then the answers
Lie with me too.

The answers lie with you
The answers lie with me
The answers lie

The Day I Met You

Well, I had a little money,
I had a little time,
I was gonna travel,
Gonna free my mind.

I was gonna sail,
Sail the seven seas,
Find a little beach,
Just to shoot the breeze.

But, like a bolt out the blue,
That's when I met you!

I was gonna write my book,
Check out all the bars,
Have a mid-life crisis
And buy the sports car.

But it all went askew
On the day I met you!

But you're not remembering
The way it went down
I can tell by your face –
And your deeply-grooved frown.

Well, I guess that it's true
I was the one chasing you!

No expensive diamond ring,
No walks down the aisle,
No crazy old in-laws,
And no forced smiles.

No thirty-year mortgage,
No prams in the hall,
No slipping in the red
With credit cards galore.

Well, I didn't have a clue
On the day I met you!

I'm guessing we've got
A different point of view –
Some old nonsense about
Me loving and begging you?

Well, I guess I can see
That's a picture of me
On bended knee!

Well, the moral of this story
And how it's gonna end:
Don't try to see
What's around the bend

It won't be the perfect life
You intended it to be,
Being single's freedom
But let me tell you, baby,
It's also misery.

Sorry

I'm sorry for the words
that I didn't say to you,
For you not thinking
everything I did was just for you;
For not making you believe
you and I were true.
And I'm sorry for the words of love...
so very few.

We came together when the sun was high
And with heavy wings we tried to fly.
Sometimes we would soar;
Other times we would fall.

Like two spinning discs out of sync
We were always just on the brink
Of flying together through the air
Or smashing down in despair.

So, I'm sorry for the words
that I didn't say to you,
For you not thinking everything I did
was just for you;
For not making you believe
you and I were true,
And I'm sorry for the words of love...
so very few.

And if this road that you are on
Turns out not to be the one,
Then keep me not so far away
And I will heal your broken heart,
one day.

'Cause I'm sorry for the words
that I didn't say to you,
For you not thinking everything I did
was just for you,
For not making you believe
You and I were true;
And I'm sorry that my words of love.....
so very few.

The Skies in Our Lives
(They Are no Longer Blue)

Do you remember
what I once said to you?
"Careful what you wish for it
may just come true."

Now I see you
standing by the water's edge,
and I'm walking
much too close to the ledge.

So, it comes as no surprise
to me or to you,
the skies in our lives
they are no longer blue.

And whatever our mistakes
it is never too late,
to find our own way
And make our own fate.

There can be no regrets
loving is never wrong.
Both of us were weak,
thinking the other
so strong.

Do you remember
how those days used to be?
Just beautiful sunshine and not
a cloud to see.

Now I see you,
finally crossing the floor,
While I'm all alone
As you're closing the door.

Time to run for cover:
it's rain for me and you,
for the skies in our lives
they are no longer blue.

Page

First lines

Acknowledgements

I would like to give thanks to the following people:

To my foster Mother and Father, Katherine and
Earnest Dolman, now deceased. They took me in and
shared their goodness and values and saved my life.
In the 23 years I lived with them I felt loved and
developed a deeper self-worth than I might never
have done had they not opened their hearts and
home. My foster sister, Angela and brother, Michael,
for their acceptance, generosity of spirit and support
throughout my life. None of my immediate foster
family are alive today, they will never be forgotten,
but I also wish to acknowledge the continued love
and support of their children and grandchildren.

Karen O'Hagan, who witnessed the birth of much of
this collection and was loving, kind and nurturing.

To the great friends I have had throughout my life
including Tutvinder Mann who, through his acceptance
and time given, taught me emotional intelligence and
gave me an insight of how a favoured and much-loved
child could grow into a well-rounded and grounded
man. Henryk Piotrowski, who taught me the honour
to be found in duty and helped to vindicate our
shared belief that music and the arts are the balm that
soothes the grazed life.

My oldest friend Martin Morris, who always got chosen to play kiss chase by the girls in the playground at age 5 and the school football team at 14. You were always my hero, the 'older brother' I looked up to... and still do.

To Matthew Kemp who has always been supportive and complimentary toward me. You showed interest in my writing and offered inspiring praise, even going to the length of having one poem recited and recorded for my benefit, thus providing me with further motivation to continue.

To Geoff French, another recently fallen warrior of the heart. A beautiful man with a beautiful soul.

To Fred and Denise Smithers who, through their generous encouragement and support, are largely responsible for enabling me to not only start but also to finish these creative efforts.

Rebecca Nichols, Becca Lethlean and Celia Wells who helped with editing and proofing but also gave fulsome praise for my efforts.

And finally, I would like to thank all the people who have entered my life so far and have either stayed or left. Without that enrichment and ever so human interaction I would have had such little inspiration for this collection. Whether I added to your life or not, I thank you profoundly for adding to mine.

ISBN:
978-1-7392664-0-0

(97)8-1-7392664-0-0

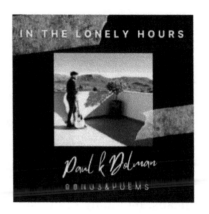

Find the album on Bandcamp
https://paulkdolman.bandcamp.com

Follow Paul K Dolman on:

Instagram.   **YouTube**

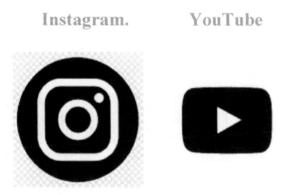

Milton Keynes UK
Ingram Content Group UK Ltd.
UKHW020942280823
427620UK00017B/1080

9 781739 266400